CU00696889

Driving Test Secre

Maria McCarthy

Driving Test Secrets You Need to Know

Find the right instructor, overcome nerves, impress your examiner on the big day and drive alone confidently

ISBN Paperback - 978-1-7384529-0-3
ISBN ebook - 978-1-7384529-1-0

A catalogue record for this book is available from the British Library.

IMPORTANT NOTE TO READERS
This book has been written and published for informational and
educational purposes only.
Any use of information in this book is at the readers' discretion and risk.
The author cannot be held responsible for any loss, claim or damage
arising out of the use or misuse of the suggestions made. No liability is
assumed by the author the reader is entirely responsible for his or her
own actions.

ABOUT THE AUTHOR
Maria McCarthy is a motoring journalist writing for national magazines
and newspapers. She also broadcasts on motoring matters and has
appeared on BBC Breakfast, Sky, ITN and carried out over 2000 radio
interviews. She is also the author of The Girls' Guide to Losing Your L
Plates and The Girls' Car Handbook published by Simon and Schuster.

Book cover and interior design – Design for Writers

Contents

CHAPTER 1:

EVERYTHING IS HARD BEFORE IT IS EASY, INCLUDING LEARNING TO DRIVE

Having a driving licence is wonderful and gives you freedom and flexibility. However actually passing your driving test can be expensive, time-consuming and nerve-wracking. It's my heartfelt wish that *Driving Test Secrets you Need to Know* will make the process smoother and easier for you.

Who am I and why should you take my advice?

I'm a motoring journalist who has been flown to exotic locations to test-drive sports cars, written for national newspapers and magazines and carried out thousands of radio and TV interviews on motoring topics. But do you know what? I struggled to pass my own driving test. I made virtually every mistake you can think of including sticking with driving instructors I wasn't suited to and succumbing to driving test nerves.

Finally I had one of the most joyful days of my life. I passed my driving test! I went on to enjoy the fun and independence of motoring. But over time I reflected on the sometimes rocky road to gaining my licence and realised that if only I'd been aware of potential pitfalls and known a few simple hacks it could have been far less stressful and taken a lot less time and money. That prompted me to write my first book, *The Girls' Guide to Losing your L Plates* published by Simon and Schuster. The reviews and responses were overwhelmingly positive with readers saying how much the combination of practical advice and emotional support had helped them pass their own driving tests.

When writing *Driving Test Secrets* I wanted to create a book that could help both male and female learner drivers of all ages and nationalities. This book uses the UK test and driving regulations as background but I've written it with the aim of helping readers worldwide. Because although the regulations and formats of driving tests varies between different countries and States, the basic principles of passing your driving test remain the same. They include finding an excellent instructor, keeping a positive outlook during the ups, downs and plateaus of the learning process and staying focused and confident during your test.

To explain the *Secrets* part of the title I should clarify that I'm not going to be suggesting anything shady or revealing Jedi mind-tricks that will influence your examiner into giving you a positive test result. It's more that I want to unravel a lot of the myths and misconceptions around learning to drive and empower you to make clear, grounded choices.

Everything is hard before it is easy – and that includes learning to drive

Although one day driving will be easy for you, when you're a learner it's pretty much guaranteed that some aspects of it are going to be hard. To earn that coveted licence you'll need to:

Become a capable driver

Some people pick up driving skills very quickly. They tend to be naturally good at judging speed and distance, have an excellent sense of spatial relationships and are confident when interacting with other road users. However, most of us don't fit into that category, finding at least some aspects hard or frustrating, whether that's struggling to get the hang of reversing or initially feeling fearful on fast roads. This book doesn't cover the practicalities of learning to drive as that's something for a qualified professional to teach. However it will guide you through one of the most important decisions of your learning to drive journey in Chapter 2 Finding the right driving instructor.

For learners finding mastering the skills involved in driving a manual car overwhelming, it's worth considering learning in an automatic. Getting to grips with gear changes and clutch control will no longer be an issue. Switching can be a game-changer for nervous drivers and anyone who struggles with co-ordination. The pros and cons of this decision are covered in Chapter 4, Is an automatic the answer?

Ride the emotional roller coaster

The extent to which learning to drive can be a very emotional experience isn't generally acknowledged. The assumption is that you'll have some lessons, do a bit of deep breathing to calm you down on test day and that's that. But many learners experience far more turbulent feelings. Including, but not limited to, the embarrassment of messing up yet another parallel park, the shame of taking longer to pass than your family and friends and the sweaty-palmed anxiety of driving test nerves. And that's even before we get onto the stress about how much the whole process is costing.

Stay financially savvy

As we're all aware, learning to drive is hugely expensive, so you'll need to budget for it. Even if you're a naturally skilled driver who feels they won't need that many lessons you could be in for an unpleasant shock. The standard needed to pass the driving test has been raised over the years, to reflect busier and more complex road conditions. So don't make the common mistake of using the number of lessons your parents or older relatives took as a guideline for how many you're likely to need.

You can reduce how much it will cost you to learn to drive in a number of ways. One of the most important is to find an instructor you 'click' with. Studies have shown that people absorb information more effectively when they are relaxed, so learning with an instructor with excellent teaching skills who you also feel comfortable with is key. And you've got to be willing to move on if necessary. Staying with an instructor who's not a good fit and isn't helping you progress is one of the most common and also one of the biggest financial mistakes learners can make.

It's also vital to avoid any instructors who engage in shady practices, such as claiming to be fully qualified when they're not or getting you to drive the previous learner home during your lesson.

Having private practice in your own or a family member's car can reduce the number of lessons you'll need and build your confidence behind the wheel. However you'll have to make sure you're properly insured and are following the regulations outlined by the Driver and Vehicle Licensing Agency (DVLA).

Another huge money-drain is having to take your test more than once. In the UK the practical test fee is currently £62. Add on the cost of extra lessons to maintain your skills and taking another test in your driving instructor's car and the bill can run into hundreds of pounds.

The current first-time pass rate in the UK is 48% - meaning 52% of candidates return home disappointed. If your driving instructor has put you forward for your test it means they believe you are good enough to pass. However being let down by driving test nerves is a real possibility and the reason for many failures. Tips on overcoming them are covered in Chapter 3 Mindset matters and Chapter 6 How to get your driving test off to a flying start. There's additional advice on how to ensure things go smoothly on the big day in Chapter 7 How to impress your driving examiner.

Learning to drive can initially appear a daunting process. But the hard work and financial outlay involved is totally offset by the joy of finally gaining your driving licence. You'll be able to take pride in having acquired a valuable skill that will bring you freedom, access to new career and social opportunities and stand you in good stead for the rest of your life.

Throughout *Driving Test Secrets* you'll be reading about other learner drivers' journeys on their way to test success. Here are just a few examples:

I had a few lessons at 17 which went exceptionally badly. In the final one I accidentally scraped my instructor's car, she shouted at me and I cried. Learning to drive became one of those things I knew I should do but kept putting off. I always had an excuse. Initially it was because I couldn't afford it. Then I got a better paid job and my new excuse was that I didn't have time. But the truth was I was worried any future attempts would be a replay of my early driving lesson disasters. A few years ago I wanted to change my career to one where I'd need a driving licence so I had no choice but to get on with it. I can't say learning to drive was a breeze but it wasn't as bad as I'd feared it would be either – finding a kind and supportive instructor made all the difference. I passed on my second attempt and it was such a relief to have finally gained such a useful qualification. *Millie, 26*

I wanted to learn to drive for as long as I can remember. As a child I used to beg my mum to let me do small things like use the key fob to open the car door. I even had dreams where I was driving. I was so lucky because I found the right instructor straight away and was able to practise in the family car at weekends, but I do realise that it's not so easy for everyone. *Sasha, 17*

I've always loved cars and wanted to learn to drive as soon as possible but lessons and the test are so expensive. I'd saved birthday and

Christmas money but that got used up very quickly. I took a weekend job and my mum chipped in, but it was still a real stretch. My mum is a single parent and can't drive, so she didn't have any experience to guide me. When I was over at a friend's house I mentioned that my driving instructor made me drive the previous learner home. His dad overheard and said that was wrong and the instructor was taking advantage. He said the whole lesson should be spent teaching and not using me as a taxi service. I ditched that instructor and got a new one. When all my time was spent practising manoeuvres and getting out onto the dual carriageway rather than driving round local streets I made much better progress and passed quickly. *Ashley, 18*

My older cousin said to me, 'Learning to drive will take longer, be more difficult and cost more money than you think'. I didn't take it too seriously as I'm good with mechanical things and felt confident. But actually he was right. I'd thought I could just go out practising with my dad and have a few extra top-up lessons. But my instructor explained that it takes way more than that these days to get to test standard. I failed my first test for moving out too quickly at a junction. Then I missed my second test because of being delayed and turning up late – but I still had to pay for it. I passed the third, but getting my licence cost far more than I thought it would. *Fergus, 20*

To say I'm not a natural driver would be a massive understatement. When I asked my final instructor (I went through quite a few) if he thought I'd ever make it he said it would take a lot of time and effort but he believed I was capable. Then added, 'I'm not saying it's going be easy, but I am saying it's going to be worth it'. He was right. Being able to drive is wonderful. I love the freedom of being able to take off at a moment's notice and not worry about booking trains or waiting for the bus. I've been quite successful in my professional life but one of the achievements I'm most proud of is passing my driving test. *Chloe, 42*

CHAPTER 2:

HOW TO FIND THE RIGHT DRIVING INSTRUCTOR

As a motoring journalist and author I've done countless radio and TV interviews on the topic of learning to drive. I'm often asked, 'What's your best tip for new learners?' And my reply is always the same, 'Find the right instructor. Do that, and everything else will fall into place. If you try to learn with someone who's not a good fit for you then the whole process will take longer, cost more and be way more stressful'.

There are lots of reasons why finding the right instructor is so important. Here are just a few:

The unfamiliar nature of one-to-one tuition

At school most of us are taught in classes of around 30 and even sports coaching tends to happen in small groups. Having an instructor focus totally on you can feel uncomfortable initially.

I was always the kid who sat at the back of the class and tried to avoid the teacher's attention. I hated being asked to read things out or contribute to a discussion. I'd much rather try and work things out for myself. I took driving lessons at 17 but struggled

because I felt so self-conscious and whenever my instructor corrected me I'd feel as
if I was being 'told off'. So I gave up for
a few years. When I went back, I'd gone
through catering college, was working as a
chef and felt a lot more confident. Although
the one-to-one tuition still felt awkward I
was mature enough to be able to deal with
it that time round. *Alex, 22*

During the driving lesson you and your instructor are
stuck in a metal box together, facing forwards and without the opportunity for eye contact whilst also dealing
with potentially stressful situations such as negotiating a
complex junction. Basically the interior of a car isn't the
ideal learning environment so it really helps if you get on
with the person you're sharing it with.

Your driving instructor will probably see you at your worst – and at your best!

Do you have a tendency to get frustrated when things
aren't going your way? Or maybe you become tearful?
Perhaps you retreat into yourself, give up hope and stop
trying?

Whatever glitches there are in your character there's a
pretty good chance your driving instructor will get to see
them as you experience the ups and downs of the learning
process. And that's even before they're called upon to coach
you through driving test day nerves.

But they will also get to see how fantastic you are too.
Apart from the lucky few who are natural drivers, learning
to drive takes a lot of hard work and determination and

high-quality instructors very much respect their students' efforts as well as their eventual success.

The need to have open and honest communication

Obviously your driving instructor needs to be able to explain new driving skills in a way that helps you understand them. But there's a lot more to instructor-pupil communication than that. It's a two-way street and you need to be comfortable telling them your thoughts and feelings as well.

Maybe you've received upsetting news shortly before your lesson. You're feeling wobbly but then your instructor suggests spending time on something you find challenging, such as tackling a busy dual carriageway. If you don't feel up to it you've got to be willing to say so and suggest that you practise something else. Also if you've been taught a particular manoeuvre but a few lessons later have completely forgotten it, you've got to be able to feel OK about admitting that to your instructor. This is a perfectly normal phenomenon by the way. It's part of the 'learning plateau' – that stage of absorbing a new skill where you've got some grasp of it, but it's not yet become fully automatic. You'll have gone through this process with everything you've ever learned, from tying your shoelaces to getting the hang of a new piece of tech. But to move past the plateau you've got to give honest feedback to your instructor about what you do and don't currently understand.

I always say to my learners that there's no such thing as a stupid question. If you don't understand something the most sensible thing to do is to ask. Sometimes the first way I explain a driving skill might not work for a particular learner so I see it as my job to find different ways until we reach one that 'clicks' for them. *Danielle 56, driving instructor*

I feel pleased when my learners ask me 'stupid questions' because it shows that they trust me enough to know I won't be sarcastic or impatient with them. *Ravi 43, driving instructor*

SO HOW DO YOU FIND THE RIGHT DRIVING INSTRUCTOR?

Firstly reflect on what sort of instructor might suit you. At the end of this chapter there's a round-up of learner-instructor partnerships that worked out brilliantly. It illustrates what an individual choice it is and how having a clear idea of the qualities you're looking for can be so helpful. Do you want an instructor who is patient, or one that will push you? Someone older or about your own age? Maybe you couldn't handle being taught by someone who supports a rival football team? Like I say, it's a very personal choice and the clearer you are about what you want at the outset the better.

A large school or an independent?

There are big driving school chains that operate across the UK, and also smaller companies with several driving instructors that work in a particular geographical area. The advantage of going with a larger school is that they often offer services such as online bookings and can arrange cover if an instructor is unable to work because of illness or annual leave. You're more likely to get an instructor you are assigned rather than one you choose, though with some schools if you want a particular instructor that you've heard about through family or friends you can request them in advance.

The advantage of going with an independent instructor is a more personal service. Also, independent instructors have to work hard to build their reputation to find students as they won't have a well-known brand name behind them. But ultimately, it's not about whether you choose a large school or an independent one – it's the relationship you have with your instructor that's the most important factor.

Location

The vast majority of pupils will want to be picked up from their work or home. Initially your lessons will be carried out on quiet streets. But as your confidence grows you'll be tackling busier roads and becoming familiar with test centre routes. If you live in a town with a test centre then that's very convenient. However, if you're in a rural area you might face a long drive to get to those routes, maybe along undemanding roads that don't give you the opportunity to improve your skills. Learners in this situation sometimes decide to get a lift or take public transport into the nearest large town or city and be picked up by their instructor from there. It's less convenient but also means that you'll be making better use of the time (and money) that you are spending on your driving instructor.

I live in a town 30 minutes outside Carlisle, where my local test centre is based. I work in the city and had my driving lessons straight after work so I could do busier routes rather than waste time driving along country roads from my home. *Jacob, 42*

I wanted to start learning to drive as soon as I turned 17. Driving instructors would wait outside the school for their pupils and as one of the youngest in my year I'd already seen my mates be collected and how some of the other kids would jeer at them as they drove off. I'd already had a hard time with bullies and I didn't want to give them another opportunity to have a go at me so although it would have been more convenient to be picked up at school I had my instructor collect me from my house. *Dan, 17*

Are they an ADI or PDI?

ADI stands for Approved Driving Instructor and they should display a green badge sticker in their window. PDI stands for Potential Driving Instructor and they will have a pink one. ADIs will have passed three exams. The first two will have assessed their driving ability and knowledge of the Highway Code. The third will have been the Instructional Ability Test after which successful candidates are awarded their teaching certificate. PDIs will have passed the first two exams but are still working towards the third. This means they have proved themselves to be very capable drivers but their teaching skills have not yet been officially validated. PDIs are at a stage of their training where they are legally allowed to teach learners, but not set up their own company - they have to work within an established driving school. During this time, they are allowed three attempts at their teaching certificate. If they repeatedly fail they are no longer allowed to work as a PDI. Obviously, lesson costs with a PDI should be lower than with an ADI.

Unfortunately, there are driving schools that will assign a PDI to a learner driver without telling them that this is not a fully qualified instructor. Always ask if your instructor is an ADI or PDI and check their badge and its expiry date before taking a lesson. Whether you go the ADI or PDI route is up to you, but what's important is that you are making a fully informed choice.

ADI grading

ADI will have what's called a 'Standards Check' every four years. During this an examiner will observe them giving a 45 minute lesson and will assess them in the categories of lesson planning, risk management and teaching and learning skills, and give appropriate marks. 0-30 is a fail, 31-42 is a Grade B and 43-51 is a Grade A, which represents the highest standard of instruction. Although you can ask an ADI about their grading, it's important to bear in mind that it's just a snapshot of a particular lesson on a particular day and not a definitive marker of their skills. Many ADIs will move between an A and B Grade and back again throughout their career. So although it's something to be aware of, what really matters is the rapport that you feel with a potential instructor.

Do they offer additional support?

All driving instructors should be supportive. However, there are driving instructors who have greater experience in teaching learners with additional needs, such as those with physical challenges or who are neurologically diverse. If there are charities or support groups related to your specific issue then do contact them as they may be able to help with information and advice and some may have a register of suitable instructors.

When it comes to nervous drivers, many driving instructors will state on their website that they can support them but this is an instance where the personal connection between you is especially important, so be sure to chat beforehand to get a feel for whether a particular instructor is one that you'll feel comfortable with.

What type of car?

Most learners will want a manual licence and so will need to learn to drive in a manual car. Their manual licence will then qualify them to drive both manual and automatic cars. However, some might prefer to take lessons in an automatic car because it's quicker and easier even though they will only be qualified to drive automatic cars after passing their test. I go into this decision in more depth in Chapter 4, Is an automatic the answer? so check that out if you're currently undecided.

Outside of that decision, learner driver cars tend to be of a particular type – small, reliable, fuel-efficient motors such as the VW Polo or Toyota Yaris. Opportunities to learn on an electric car are increasing all the time as more instructors offer them. However, as they don't have gears you will only gain an automatic licence.

When you've passed your test, part of becoming a confident driver is learning to adapt to driving different vehicles so the particular make or model of car an instructor uses shouldn't be a deciding factor. Choosing the right person is far more important than their vehicle. Having said that, if you're unsure and one driving school has a car that particularly appeals to you or is similar to one you're practising on or hoping to buy then you can let that be the deciding factor.

Don't focus too much on a driving school's 'First-Time Pass Rate'

Some instructors will very much highlight their high 'first-time pass rate'. Of course, everyone wants to pass first time so this can be very appealing. But it's important to bear in mind that driving schools tend to have different clientele. Some will be mostly teaching young, able learners. Those are the driving school cars you'll see parked up outside your local 6th form college waiting to pick up 17-year-old pupils for their lessons. And as younger people tend to pick up driving skills more easily than older ones this means their first-time pass rate is likely to be much higher than that of a school which specialises in older or nervous drivers or those with special needs.

The cost of lessons and bookings procedure

Learning to drive is an expensive process. According to the Driver Vehicle and Licensing Agency (DVLA) the average learner needs 45 hours of driving lessons in addition to 20 hours of private practice. Obviously that's going to vary depending on your level of aptitude but given the cost of lessons can range between £25-55 you're looking at between £1125 - £2475 for tuition.

Learners often feel upset at how expensive lessons can be, but it's important to also see things from the instructor's perspective. It's not just about the cost of their time. Instructors also have to insure and maintain their vehicle, pay for fuel and various forms of insurance and also cover the periods they spend travelling between pupils.

There are a number of factors that influence how much an instructor charges and one of the most significant is their experience and how popular they are. The reputation of the best instructors tends to spread by word of mouth and they are more likely to have long waiting lists and be able to charge higher prices. Lower prices might indicate an instructor who is struggling to get pupils. However, there's the chance that a cheaper instructor may be newly qualified but very keen and a good instructor for you. The only way to find that out is to chat to them. Discover how long they've been teaching and aim to get a feel for why they might be so inexpensive.

It can also be worth checking out how your instructor's booking system works. Do you book in lessons in person, over the phone or via their website? Having clarity about that will help if you ever need to change or cancel lessons. Incidentally, it's worth pointing out that many instructors don't offer 1 hour lessons, just 1.5 or 2 hour ones – so that's something to discuss with them at the outset. Overall, it's best to have 2 hour lessons if you can as it will give you more of a chance to settle into the drive and also to go further afield and experience different types of roads. If you'd rather have lessons early in the morning, after work or at weekends, then clarify that with any potential instructors and check their availability.

Driving instructors often offer discounts for block bookings. It works for them as it helps them plan their budget and it can offer good value for you too. However I'd advise delaying them initially. Block bookings tie you in with an instructor for a significant number of lessons (normally at least 10 or 20) and if you decide for whatever reason you're not a good fit and want to try another instructor that won't be possible until you've either used up your 'block' or passed your test (in which case the unused lessons should be refunded).

Wait until you're sure you've found an instructor you want to stick with before committing to block bookings and then do go ahead and take advantage of the savings.

Personal recommendation

So having considered the various factors it's time to draw up a list of potential instructors. Personal recommendation can be one of the best routes to finding a high-quality instructor. However what it doesn't take into account is our personal differences. An instructor who is perfect for a nervous driver may make a confident one feel bored and impatient. The instructor that your friend Freya thought was amazing might remind you of your annoying Aunt Alice who is always asking you why you haven't got a boyfriend yet. Or the guy with the excellent first time pass rate who taught your brother could end up irritating you by his tendency to talk too much about golf.

Checking out reviews and social media

Lots of driving instructors are on social media these days – mostly posting photos of triumphant ex-pupils brandishing their pass certificates. Reading reviews and feedback from previous students can be helpful, but it's even better when instructors post videos of themselves talking about driving, because then you pick up more of a vibe about what they're really like.

It's good to talk – or better still, have a video call

Even if you normally prefer text or messaging I'd very much urge you to arrange a call or video chat with potential instructors. It'll give you the opportunity to talk through any concerns and also to get a sense of what they're like as people and whether you might click with them.

Have a trial lesson

Chatting online or over the phone is useful for narrowing down the list of potential candidates, but it's not until you meet your instructor in person and have a trial lesson with them that you'll really know whether you're going to click. So go down the trial lesson route, perhaps with a few instructors and continue with the one you feel is best suited to you.

A few red flags to watch out for

If possible it's advised to stick with the same instructor throughout your learning to drive journey. But if the relationship isn't working out then it's best to move on – and also preferable if that can happen sooner rather than later, before too much time and energy has been invested. Here are a few pointers to help you spot an unsuitable instructor.

Illegal 'driving instructors'

Some unscrupulous individuals set up as 'driving instructors' while having no qualifications whatsoever whilst others are PDIs who have repeatedly failed the teaching section of their training but have continued to take out learners. It's unsafe to learn with these people and if there's an accident neither of you will be covered by insurance. Ensure you are learning with a genuine ADI or PDI by checking their details on the DVLA database.

Unprofessional behaviour

If your driving instructor behaves unprofessionally, for example shouting, swearing, making inappropriate remarks, initiating unnecessary physical contact or using their mobile phone when you are driving you should terminate your lessons with them and ask for a refund for any block bookings. You may also wish to report them to the DVLA.

Short-changing

Avoid instructors who turn up late then finish the lesson on time without any promise of making the difference up later. Also, ones who want you to drive the previous learner home at the start of your lesson, or to pick a new one up at the end. All of the lesson should be focused on you and your needs – you're not a taxi service!

Too much talk and not enough driving

Driving is something you learn through doing, not discussion. Sometimes an instructor will need you to park up so they can explain some aspect of driving. But there are instructors that do this far more than necessary in an attempt to save on fuel. It's not a productive way to spend your lessons so find a different instructor.

Shady practices

Watch out for any lack of transparency around pricing For example, some driving schools might really promote super-cheap 'introductory lessons' on their website whilst doing their best to conceal that the price shoots up after that. And check how long a 'lesson' lasts – we tend to assume that a lesson is one hour, but some schools might try to pass off 45 minutes as 'a lesson'.

Avoid any instructors of schools that show a lack of honesty about whether they are are offering you an ADI or a PDI. That's something they need to be completely upfront about. Also be aware of the fact that there have been instances of some driving schools taking money for block bookings and then not providing the lessons for whatever reason. If possible pay for lessons by credit card so you have the opportunity to make a claim under Section 75 of the Consumer Credit Act if there is a breach of contract.

PERFECT PARTNERSHIPS

I'm aware that the steps involved in finding the right driving instructor can feel overwhelming. But speaking as someone who personally had to go through a few instructors before finding my ideal, believe me when I say it's totally worth it.

When you're learning to drive, you and your instructor form a partnership. Its purpose is for you to become a safe driver for life and to pass your driving test with flying colours. The best partnerships are those where the people involved have the right chemistry. When you just 'click' it makes any goal or challenge easier. Here are a few examples of some fantastic partnerships. As you'll see, it's about finding the right fit between learner and instructor. For example the instructor that was perfect for Rowan wouldn't have suited Maura. When researching driving instructors put the time in to find your own perfect match – you'll be so glad you did!

Sasha and Emily

Emily made learning to drive a fun experience. She had a relaxed, upbeat manner and never got stressed so I didn't either. Emily was very good at explaining things in different ways. If I didn't 'get it' one way, she'd try another until I finally understood. She also didn't get annoyed if I forgot things between lessons. She said it was part of the learning process and that everything would fall into place eventually. Emily was in her twenties and we'd have chats about music and clothes. I felt at ease with her in a way that I wouldn't have with someone who felt too 'grown-up' and I think that helped me learn more easily. *Sasha, 17*

Maura and Ravi

I went to a strict school with a hyper-competitive 'hot-housing' approach and I hated every minute of it. I knew I wanted kind, patient tuition and was lucky enough to find Ravi. It was like having a wise, supportive uncle who was also a brilliant driving instructor. *Maura, 25*

Jacob and Danielle

As a man in his early 40s learning to drive I wanted an instructor who wasn't going to judge me for not picking the skills up as easily as a 17 year old. I also wanted a mature instructor as I would have felt awkward being taught by someone in their 20s. Danielle was perfect as she was in her 50s and explained everything really well. Even when I had a bad day and it felt as though I'd forgotten everything she'd ever taught me I always felt Danielle had my back and believed I'd get there in the end. *Jacob, 42*

Rowan and Callum

I was already an experienced motorcyclist and confident on the roads long before I began taking driving lessons. I wanted an instructor who would set high standards for both of us and who would get me through my test as soon as possible. I contacted Callum who was ex-Marines and took no prisoners! Once he worked out what I was capable of and what I wanted we both agreed that we would work hard, concentrate on any problem areas and keep going until we fixed them. Going over and over manoeuvres I found difficult was frustrating and stressful at times, but staying focused paid off. I passed first time with no minors! I'm very grateful to Callum for his teaching skills and commitment. *Rowan, 23*

So you've got your driving instructor sorted. Now it's time to get you into the most positive state of mind possible for the journey between where you are now and who you want to become – a fully licensed, safe and confident driver.

CHAPTER 3:

MINDSET MATTERS

Some challenging experiences, such as ongoing dental work can be got through in a spirit of endurance. Another person (the dentist) is doing all the hard work and your job is to sit there and let them get on with it. But it's not like that with learning to drive. No matter how fantastic and empathic your driving instructor is they can't do it all for you. Don't underestimate what a huge difference your own attitude and commitment makes.

In my family driving lessons are the automatic 17th birthday gift. But I just wasn't ready. I hated everything about learning to drive and when my instructor rang on the doorbell I used to feel sick. I'd grit my teeth, get through the lesson and then bounce out of the car thinking, 'at least that's over for another week'. Needless to say I didn't make much progress and didn't get anywhere near test-ready. I went away to university and didn't give learning to drive another thought until I was in my early thirties. My husband and I had moved to the countryside and were planning to start a family and no way did I want to be hauling buggies around on the bus. This time round my attitude was totally different. I wasn't a natural driver but I was determined to crack it. I took as many lessons as we could afford, was always upfront with my instructor about what was and wasn't working for me and went out for practice drives with my husband every chance I got. It took me four attempts to pass but I got there in the end and I've been a safe driver ever since. *Jenny, 37*

I changed driving instructors six times. Looking back, I now realise I was hoping to find someone with a mysterious super-power that would enable them to magically transfer their top-notch driving abilities to me without any effort on my part. It never worked and I might as well have stuck with the first one. I've come to the conclusion that driving instructors are like husbands. You always think it would be better with someone else's, but in the end they're all the same. *Chloe, 42*

To get the best value out of your driving lessons you have to show up for them open and willing to learn. That means communicating with your driving instructor about how you're feeling and what you do and don't understand and also spending time outside your lessons building up your knowledge about driving. This latter aspect is covered in Chapter 5, Always Be Learning.

However as well as practical strategies there is also inner work to be done. Almost every learner has had times when they've felt overwhelmed by how much there is to understand or dispirited after a difficult lesson. It's easy to descend into a miserable spiral, telling yourself that you're alone in finding driving so hard and even being tempted by the thought of abandoning your lessons.

Be Kind – to yourself

I'm about to offer you a variety of strategies to build up your confidence and self-belief but before that I want to begin by urging you to be kind to the very person it's most difficult for you to be kind to – yourself. It's entirely possible that during the process of learning to drive you will:

- make mistakes (often the same mistakes, repeatedly)
- be frustrated
- cry during a lesson (no shame, I did this myself!)
- feel you're letting your driving instructor down
- worry about how much money learning to drive is costing you (or your parents)
- feel inadequate when comparing yourself to family and friends who learned quickly and easily

All these situations and feelings are perfectly normal.

I'd always been academic and good at written exams so I'd come to see myself as someone who picked things up easily. When it came to driving I couldn't have been more wrong! I kept forgetting the sequence I was meant to do things in when operating the car. I also realised how poor my sense of spatial relationships must be as all my various instructors kept telling me off for driving too close to the centre of the road when I was convinced we were near the pavement. Standing at the bus stop in my thirties watching teenagers drive past knowing that they'd managed to achieve something I was struggling with was a very humbling experience. *Chloe, 42*

All my friends at school breezed through their driving tests but it took me ages. I felt ashamed of how difficult I found driving and it was embarrassing to admit I was still learning long after my mates had got their licences. *Kira, 19*

Learning to drive might feel hard at times but don't make it more stressful by being hard on yourself. I'm not going to deny that the cost of lessons and tests really dials up the pressure. But worrying is counter-productive. Studies have shown that people learn best when they're relaxed because their brains are more open to receiving new information. So, cutting yourself some slack and doing what you can to lower your stress levels will actually mean you'll learn more effectively and need fewer lessons.

As much as you are able, aim to lighten up about the process of learning to drive and forgive yourself for the inevitable mistakes made along the way. Talking your feelings and anxieties through with supportive family and friends can help you gain a sense of perspective. Time spent with pets is a guaranteed mood changer. Walk your dog or play with your cat before and after a lesson and remind yourself that they love you unconditionally and couldn't care less that you can't do a reverse park yet.

SET YOURSELF UP FOR SUCCESS

Here are some suggestions to help you develop a positive and resilient attitude and pass your driving test more easily.

Learn to meditate

Suggesting meditation is one of the most unpopular pieces of advice it is possible to give. Almost everyone claims that they 'can't meditate' because they find it difficult to block out unwanted thoughts. But it's important to realise that we all face exactly the same challenge. Hermits who have spent years in caves up a mountainside training themselves to tune out all distractions still end up wondering about what they'll have for breakfast, so you're not alone.

Meditation is like going to the gym in that the benefits accumulate over time. You can initially use meditation techniques to help calm you before your driving lessons. Then by the time then by the time your driving test rolls round you'll be more confident in your ability to dial down your nerves.

There's a wide variety of approaches to meditation. Experiment with different types and see if you can find one that works for you.

Observe your breath – this is one of the simplest forms. You can begin by setting a timer for five or ten minutes and just quietly focus on your breath. When other thoughts start to intrude (as they inevitably will), let them come and go without getting particularly attached, and bring your focus back to your breath.

Repeat a mantra - choose a particular phrase, such as 'I feel calm' and slowly repeat it to yourself

Use a guided meditation – there are lots of guided meditations available via apps and on YouTube. They can be the best place to start if you are new to meditation.

Use affirmations and visualisation

As you're probably already aware top athletes use affirmations and visualisation to help them reach their peak performance. The more they 'affirm' or 'see' themselves being first across the finish line or scoring the winning goal the more attainable that goal will appear and the more likely they are to achieve it in reality.

These techniques work for other areas of life as well, including learning to drive. There's no shortage of books and videos available describing how to use affirmations and visualisations and they are definitely worth checking out, to learn more and deepen your understanding.

Affirmations

Affirmations usually involve writing, thinking or stating your preferred reality in the present tense as if it's already happening. For example, 'my driving is getting better all the time'. There are lots of options for getting the most out of this practise including posting your affirmations where you'll see them and frequently saying, singing or reflecting on them. So if you're out for a run or waiting in a supermarket queue you might like to choose a favourite affirmation and just repeat it to yourself quietly in your mind.

The best affirmations are ones you create yourself because you'll resonate with them better. You'll know you've found one that works because there will be a sense of it 'clicking' with you and you'll sense a positive shift (however small) as you repeat or write it. When you're first learning you can set the bar fairly low, with affirmations such as 'my driving is improving all the time' and as you get closer to your test you can upgrade them to ones such as 'I am ready to pass my test' and 'I am ready to drive alone'.

Here are some sample affirmations to get you going, but the more you tweak them to suit you personally the more effective they will be.

I am becoming a good and safe driver

I'm making progress even when it feels like I'm not. My brain is integrating all the skills

I'm being taught and soon everything will just fall into place for me.

Learning to drive is fun

I am a safe and capable driver

I love driving

Visualisation

Visualisation is about imagining and 'seeing' the scenarios you want to take place in real life. You don't have to sit cross-legged on a yoga mat with incense burning to do visualisations (although of course you can if you like). It's something you can do when you're waiting for the bus, walking your dog or queuing in a cafe.

Some people find it easier to 'see' themselves in visualisations, as if they were a character in a film, whereas others prefer to tap into the emotions they'd be having. As with affirmations, visualisations work best when you personalise them to suit yourself. Here are a few suggestions.

Imagine getting out of the car after a lesson which went really well. You feel capable and proud of yourself.

Visualise a supervised driving session where you drove to a neighbouring town without any guidance or prompting required, just as a licensed driver would.

As you get closer to your driving test – visualisations can get really exciting and inspiring!

Imagine your examiner turning to you and telling you you've passed.

Visualise calling your friends and family to tell them you've got your driving licence.

Imagine you are driving alone, feeling happy and confident.

Be careful what you say, because someone very important is listening.

It's you! Even if affirmations and visualisations aren't your thing, at least make a decision not to trash-talk about your driving. Obviously if you're feeling stressed and upset then it's good to confide in your driving instructor and people close to you such as family and trusted friends. But don't get in the habit of putting yourself down, and emphasising any difficulties you have. Criticising yourself in that way is a powerful form of self-sabotage.

> I learnt to drive when I was at 6th form along with two of my closest friends. None of us were natural drivers and in breaks we'd sit around complaining about disastrous driving lessons and how hopeless we were and that we'd never pass. At the time we felt those venting sessions were helping us let off steam and to a certain extent they were. But I also think they made us dwell too much on our insecurities and we'd have done better without them. *Sabrina, 19*

Write down why you want your driving licence

We are all individuals and have our own unique motivations for doing things. For example, one person might become a doctor because they want to help others, someone else might do it to please their parents and a third could be motivated by the prospect of making megabucks via providing celebs with cosmetic surgery. Same goal, different reasons.

It's the same with learning to drive.

Why do you personally want to be able to drive? Is it so you can get to college without waiting in the rain for the bus? The freedom to just take off and visit friends at a moment's notice? Maybe you know that having a licence is essential for your chosen career?

Whatever they are, write them down and ideally pin them up somewhere you will see them regularly. Alternatively take a photo of your list with your phone and look at it whenever you feel your motivation flagging.

I'm going to study Biology at University and my dream job is to be a warden on a nature reserve like the one in Scotland we visited for our A level field trip. Obviously you can't do that without a driving licence! I had photos of the reserve as screen savers on my phone and computer and every time I had a disappointing lesson or failed a test (it took me five attempts to pass) I'd look at them and it would remind me why I was putting myself through this. *Kira, 19*

I was never interested in cars and when I lived in cities I wasn't particularly bothered about not having a driving licence. Then I moved to the Lake District, joined a hill-walking and mountaineering group and really enjoyed going out with them every weekend. They encourage car-sharing, but after a while I got embarrassed about always asking for lifts but never being able to offer any. I also wanted to get out into the beautiful countryside by myself, independent of the group. So at 40 I finally decided I had to bite the bullet and learn to drive. *Jacob, 42*

OVERCOMING DRIVING TEST FAILURE WITH A POSITIVE MINDSET

Hopefully you'll pass your test first time. But unfortunately it's possible that things just might not go your way on the day. Driving test failure is a very bruising experience and it's understandable if your initial reaction is to feel deeply upset and discouraged.

It took me several attempts to pass my driving test. The first failure was definitely the worst. I followed all the tips for success including visualising myself passing, taking Bach Rescue Remedy, and eating a banana. I set off buoyed up with confidence and returned home feeling utterly defeated, having failed for driving too close to some parked cars. The next test I felt I drove well, and thought I should have passed but unfortunately my examiner didn't share that opinion. She failed me for hesitating at a junction. My third I failed for messing up a reverse parking manoeuvre. I started to wonder if I was jinxed! Thankfully it was fourth time lucky. *Jenny, 37*

I must admit I cried when I failed my first driving test. It was my husband's birthday the following week and I'd hoped to be able to drive us down to the coast for a day out to celebrate. Normally I'm not a crier but the combination of the stress of the driving test and the disappointment of failing pushed me over the edge. I was so embarrassed but my driving instructor told me not to worry and that they see tears all the time, from both men and women. *Jane, 58*

I took a boring and stressful weekend job in a call centre to help pay for my driving lessons. When I went for my first test I was desperate to pass so I could pack it in. But I failed. Having to get up at 6am the following Saturday because I needed to earn money for more lessons was horrible. *Nathan, 25*

One of the first steps to feeling better is to remember that you're not alone – in the UK 52% of learners fail their first driving test. The next is to avoid suppressing your feelings – your mood will shift far more quickly if you just let them out. A good cry can be tremendously therapeutic as is talking things through with family and friends who you know will be supportive. If you can, spend the evening after a failed driving test doing something that will soothe and comfort you, such as ordering a takeaway and watching a favourite film.

When your next driving lesson rolls around, you and your instructor can carry out the post-match analysis of what went wrong and work together to ensure that you're successful next time.

Failure is just delayed success

Although failing your driving test is undeniably disappointing, frustrating and expensive, your driving dream hasn't come to an end – it's just been postponed. Your day will come! In the meantime, when your confidence has been knocked, cheesy quotations can often provide a surprising source of strength. Like affirmations, the best ones are those that you come across yourself and strike a chord with you personally. But here are a few that I hope might help.

> I really think a champion is defined not by their wins but how they can recover when they fall. *Serena Williams, tennis player*

> You always pass failure on your way to success. *Mickey Rooney, actor*

> Winning is great, sure, but if you are really going to do something in life, the secret is learning how to lose. Nobody goes undefeated all the time. If you can pick up after a crushing defeat and go on to win again, you are going to be a champion someday. *Wilma Rudolph, Olympic athlete*

You build on failure. You use it as a step-ping stone. Close the door on the past. You don't try to forget the mistakes but you don't dwell on them. Don't let it have any of your energy or any of your time or any of your space. *Johnny Cash, singer-songwriter*

Be inspired by success

Check out the final section of Chapter 8 You've passed – how to handle your first drive alone. There you'll find 16 stories of ex-learner drivers sharing their experience of driving independently for the first time. Some of them had found picking up driving skills relatively easy, whilst others struggled through setbacks and multiple test failures. But what they all have in common is that they eventually suc-ceeded and gained that coveted licence. If you're willing to put in the necessary effort and persevere, you can too. As you read the stories, you may find ones that particularly resonate with you. Maybe you're excited by the prospect of exploring the countryside, having an easier commute, or showing those who doubted you that you can be a suc-cessful driver. Take the time right now to jot down your own 'my first drive alone story', in the past tense as if it has already happened. And whether you find your learning to drive journey fairly straightforward, or whether there are challenges along the way, it's something you can always revisit to keep your motivation strong.

CHAPTER 4:

IS AN AUTOMATIC THE ANSWER?

In the UK and most of Europe manual transmissions are the most popular. However countries such as Australia, Japan, Canada and the USA have steered towards automatic vehicles. For example in the USA approximately 95% of cars are autos.

The majority of UK-based learner drivers choose to take their test in a manual car. This is because it keeps their options open. After passing they are licensed to drive a manual or automatic vehicle whilst those who take their test in an automatic can only drive an auto afterwards unless they re-take their test in a manual.

But times are changing and automatic motoring is becoming more popular. In 2022 the Driver and Vehicle Licensing Agency (DVLA) data revealed that 1.1 million of the 41 million drivers in the UK hold automatic licences – so that's around one in 40. Back in 2012 it was only 550,000. And the number of aspiring motorists choosing to go the automatic route is increasing party because of the increasing popularity of electric vehicles (EVs). As EVs are all automatic a manual licence won't be required for them.

Should you learn to drive in an automatic?

The answer to this question depends a lot on you personally and your future motoring plans. If you're a confident twenty-something who wants the flexibility of being able to drive different vehicles, such as for work or sharing family cars then having a manual licence will be important. If you're a nervous driver who has struggled with mastering gears and just wants to buy a car of their own to get around in then maybe it's simpler to take the automatic route?

Here are some pros and cons to help you decide

Pros
Automatic cars are easier to drive

When it comes to learning to drive there are two aspects. One is 'car craft', which is learning how to operate the vehicle. The other is 'road craft'. This involves reading highway signs, dealing with traffic, pedestrians and responding to different road conditions.

In a manual car the driver has to get to grips with clutch control and shifting gear in order to match it to the appropriate speed and to handle hills and junctions smoothly. In most manual cars the gears range from one to five, with the lower gears being more suitable for lower speeds and the higher gears for faster ones.

In an automatic car a lot of the decision-making process around gears is done for you. The vehicle chooses the best gear for the speed you're travelling at and also helpfully decides what gear you should be when going up or down hills. You also don't need to master clutch control, or learn how to 'find the biting point'.

So as you can see the 'car craft' aspect is much simpler in an automatic, meaning you can give more attention to what's happening on the road.

If you struggle with co-ordination or become easily flustered and distracted then learning to drive an automatic car may be a more convenient and safer option.

It's also likely to take fewer lessons so if you need to get behind the wheel as quickly and inexpensively as possible then learning on an automatic could be right for you.

The cons

Being 'auto shamed'

Manual vehicle fans say they feel that transmission gives them greater control over the vehicle and makes driving a more fun, interactive experience.

As mentioned previously if you learn in an automatic you won't be qualified to drive a manual car. Whilst you personally might be fine with that there may well be some degree of pushback from manual drivers in your family or social circle.

They might attempt to 'auto shame' you, expressing surprise or even disdain that you're going the auto route and implying that you won't be a 'real driver'. My advice? Be open-minded and listen to different opinions when you're doing your research, but once you've made your decision then neither defend it nor engage in unwanted debates. You do you.

'That one time' when you might need to drive a manual vehicle

Manual licence enthusiasts are very keen to impress upon learners that there might be 'that one time' in the future when you'll need to drive a manual vehicle and will be tortured by regret for not having the necessary driving skills. Some of them stand up to scrutiny, others don't.

In the latter category, we have the 'you might need to rent a van or hire a car on holiday' argument. And yes, you might. However most hire and rental companies have auto options available and this is increasing as electric vehicles become more popular.

And the former tends to fall into the 'emergency' category. What if you urgently needed to take a relative to hospital or escape from a zombie horde and the only vehicle available was a manual one? In this instance, yes – busted! You would feel really bad about not having the necessary driving skills. But only you can decide the likeliness of those scenarios, and whether it's worth foregoing the relative ease of acquiring your automatic licence for it.

Buying and running an automatic vehicle

Automatic vehicles can be more expensive to buy and run than manual ones. This is partly because their gearboxes are more complex than their manual equivalent. They have software inbuilt to make the gear changing decisions for you so are more complicated to design and produce.

Insurance can also be higher as, because the vehicle is more complex, repairs may be more expensive and replacement parts harder to source.

But the news is better when it comes to fuel consumption. Many autos are more economical with fuel than manual cars. This didn't always used to be the case, but now automatics have developed so they can optimise gear changes to ensure they use as little fuel as possible.

When it comes to looking at the cost of owning and buying an automatic vehicle, it's going to depend on so many factors. It's worth crunching the numbers and ensuring that you're comparing like with like. For example comparing petrol and diesel manual vehicles with their automatic counterparts and also assessing electric vehicles as an option. Then you'll have a true idea of the costs involved and will be making a decision based on facts rather than on some vague idea that 'automatics are more expensive'.

Finding an instructor who teaches in an automatic car

Once you've decided to learn to drive in automatic you'll need to find an instructor. There are more driving schools offering manual tuition than automatic but if you live in a large city you will probably be able to find automatic and electric vehicle instructors nearby. If you live in a rural area there may be fewer automatic instructors locally. However, some learners who are keen to learn on an auto will take public transport into their nearest city or town to meet up with their instructor.

Automatic instructors probably won't have as high a first-time pass rate as their manual counterparts but this is because they're more likely to be teaching learners who lack confidence, are older or who have special needs.

Taking your test in an automatic or electric car

Your test will follow exactly the same format as if you were driving a manual car. The licence you'll get when you pass will be different however. In the B (for cars) column it will have the code 78, a restriction code meaning you are forbidden from driving a car with a manual gearbox. On the plus side you'll also have codes f and k, allowing you to drive automatic tractors and mowing machines!

Upgrading from an automatic to a manual licence

If you decide to do this at a later date, brace yourself for the added expense. You'll have acquired 'road craft' skills as an automatic driver, but how long it takes for you to get to grips with gears will depend on your natural aptitude. You'll have to pay for additional lessons but won't have to re-take the theory test. When it comes to the practical driving test, hopefully you'll pass first time but if things don't go according to plan on the day don't worry. Your automatic licence remains unaffected. You won't be ceremoniously stripped of it and demoted to taking public transport again.

Thank goodness for automatics! I had repeated attempts at learning in a manual car and always gave up in despair. Switching to an auto aged 40 was a game-changer. I only wish I'd done it sooner. Learning to drive was still a struggle but at least I got there in the end. If autos didn't exist I'm not sure I'd even have a licence. *Chloe, 42*

My nan said she'd give me her old automatic Nissan Micra so I took auto lessons and passed really quickly. It was great. Some mates tried to make fun of me for not getting a full licence but I couldn't care less. *Ali, 18*

Learning to drive was really easy for me so a manual was the obvious choice. My younger sister found it harder, so she changed to auto and got her licence that way. It's all good. *Sami, 18*

I learned to drive in an auto when I was 17 because I didn't have much money for lessons and I knew it would be cheaper. Everything was fine until I started applying for work after college and the job descriptions all said I had to have a manual licence. So I had to start taking lessons again. I was confident and had good road sense by then so that was sorted but I found gears and clutch control a hassle after years of driving without them. The weirdest thing was that on my first manual test I missed an observation and got a fail. But when we got back to the test centre I was still able to drive away in my automatic car. I passed the second time. Now I work as an electrician and have to drive different company vehicles so having a manual licence is essential and gives me more options if I change jobs in the future. *Lloyd, 23*

I think it's important to honestly unpack your reasons for not going down the auto route. I knew it didn't matter whether I had a full licence or not as I'd planned to buy a car of my own and I knew I'd never have to drive other vehicles for work. I'm not the sort of person who'd ever hire a van to do removals or anything so that wasn't relevant either. A friend with an auto licence who knew I was struggling with gears grilled me about why I wasn't doing the same and the best I could come up with was, 'If I get married my husband might have a manual and it would be useful if we could drive each other's cars'. I didn't even have a boyfriend at that point! I instantly realised how silly it was to be putting myself through the stress of learning on a manual for the sake of some mythical 'husband' and his choice of vehicle. I booked auto lessons, passed my test and never looked back. Ten years on I am married, and my husband and I both drive electric cars, so no manual licence required. *Rukmini, 33*

I was 55 and had never had any interest in learning to drive but after my husband had a stroke I knew I had to. As an older learner, I never even considered attempting it in a manual car. I found a patient auto instructor and after a lot of sweat, tears and money I finally became a licensed driver. *Jane, 58*

People say they don't like automatics until they try one. Then they don't want to go back. I've got a manual licence but no way would I run a manual car. Autos are so much more relaxing to drive, especially in city traffic. *Lauren, 39*

CHAPTER 5:

ALWAYS BE LEARNING

As we're all aware, getting your licence is an expensive business. But you can make the most of your paid lessons by committing to learning as much as possible about driving and improving your skills outside of them. Taking an Always Be Learning (ABL) approach will help you integrate what your instructor is teaching you and help you become a safer and more confident driver in the long run. And best of all, the ideas and tips below won't cost you a penny. Even trying just a few will help your progress.

1. Watch driving lesson and driving tuition videos on YouTube and other platforms. There are some really great ones out there. For example Conquer Driving is a popular UK-based channel that counts many driving instructors as its fans. However, don't follow any online advice that contradicts your driving instructor's guidance as they're the one you need to trust first and foremost.

2. Make the most of being a passenger if you're driving with family, friends in a taxi, or even on the bus. Sit in the front seat if possible and watch the decisions about speed, overtaking, and pulling out at junctions that are being made. Imagine

what you would be doing in terms of observations, gear changes and so on if you were in the driving seat. It's a great opportunity to mentally practice what you've been taught without the stress of actually being at the wheel.

3.   It's surprising how much you can learn even when you're not in a vehicle. For example, if you're waiting at a bus stop near a busy junction watch how different drivers handle it. Some will do well, others not so much! This exercise is particularly helpful in that you can be totally detached. In your role of Zen-like 'observer' you become aware of what a wide range of driving abilities are out there on the road and it helps you realise that when bad drivers tailgate or cut you up, it's usually nothing personal. They're like that with everyone!

4.   If there's a particular local road, roundabout or junction that troubles you, consider 'visiting' it. Literally going there and standing by the side of the road watching how other motorists handle what you consider 'the roundabout from hell' or whatever. Maybe it's a junction with poor visibility where you have to wait ages for a safe gap and find yourself wondering if you and your driving instructor are going to end up stuck there for the rest of your natural lives. Seeing that other drivers face the same challenge and might also have to wait a while before they can pull out can help put matters in perspective.

5.   Get your family and friends to describe how they handle manoeuvres to you. Or better still, act them out in mime! Getting Uncle Harry to back around the kitchen table whilst pretending he's reversing round a corner (lots of looking over his shoulder and doing his observations, obviously) is comedy gold and can actually help if you're initially struggling with the concept of 'going backwards'.

6.   Seek out positive driving role models. Driving well isn't just about driving skill. With increasingly busy roads and stressful lives, it's also about being able to handle your emotions. Anger, impatience, and a tendency to be easily distracted can turn anyone into a dangerous driver. So, pay particular attention to how your driving instructor and drivers you admire and feel safe with drive. Often the best drivers aren't the flashy, 'cop chase in a movie' types, but the ones who get on and do it with the minimum of drama.

7.   Chat with family and friends about driving and various situations they have had to handle since passing their own test. Hearing about how they coped with driving on icy roads for the first time, or parking in a minute space in a multi-storey car park or motoring abroad will help you realise that the world isn't divided into 'novice drivers' and 'experienced ones'. Driving isn't something you tick off a checklist and think 'well, that's sorted'. It's an ability you'll be honing throughout your life.

8. Develop the skills you'll need when you're driving on your own. Find out about navigation, via sat nav, maps and signs. Learn how to fill up at a fuel station and how to do the basic car checks such as tyre pressure and windscreen washer levels.

9. This isn't strictly driving-test related but it's still very worthwhile. Start educating yourself about the various topics that you'll need to understand when you're a licensed driver. Begin to take notice of fuel prices and how they're more expensive at some locations than others. Research car insurance. Check out cars you'd like to drive once you've passed your test, ranging from cheaper options right through to your dream car, whether that's a powerful Ferrari or a cute little Fiat 500. Being a real driver spans the whole spectrum from fun stuff such as buying a fab motor to boring admin like renewing your car tax. Becoming familiar with these tasks will help you feel like a real driver before you've even passed your test.

No-one in my family has a car so I didn't have any chance to practise outside my lessons. But when I went out with my mates I'd always help navigate and look out for parking spaces. I'd also watch how they did everyday driving tasks like refuelling and pumping up their tyres. *Ashley, 18*

I found watching mock test videos on YouTube really useful. I even got a bit addicted to be honest. Seeing other learners make mistakes made me realise what I had to watch out for. And I did pass first time! *Sasha, 17*

My boyfriend and I hadn't been together long before we went on a long drive from London to the north of Scotland. It had all the components of a difficult journey, beginning with heavy traffic and complicated diversions, followed by a thunderstorm and finally navigating winding, icy rural lanes. I'd only just started lessons so wasn't able to shoulder any of the burden but I did do my best to learn from the drive ready for when I might find myself in a similar situation on my own. I wasn't just hugely impressed by the way Jake handled the challenges but also the fact that he stayed calm and good-humoured throughout. And Reader, I married him. *Millie, 26*

I learned to drive in Exeter and one of the test routes included a 'double roundabout' (voted second in a 'Most annoying Devon Roundabouts' survey in 2018). I came to think of them as 'the Pinhoe Double Roundabouts of Doom' after my instructor marked my handling of them as a fail on two of our mock tests. One afternoon before my first test I cycled over to the roundabouts and got the hang of how they worked, both by watching drivers handle them and by cycling round them several times. My first test (which I failed) didn't include them. However my second did. I navigated them perfectly and passed. *Kris, 21*

I went to a work conference about 200 miles away on the train but a colleague offered me a lift back home which I accepted. It was the most nerve-wracking journey of my life! I'd always thought of her as quite a mild-mannered woman but behind the wheel she was extremely volatile. She'd do this thing of tailgating a car, then suddenly overtaking it and pulling back in without leaving much of a gap behind her. Terrifying for all concerned. Then she'd accelerate up behind the next vehicle, tailgate them for a bit and repeat the process. The traffic was very light so there was absolutely no need to get close to other vehicles at all. Then she missed her exit at a roundabout and went round twice. Another motorist tooted his horn and she swore at him, using shockingly bad language. By this point we were on a dual carriageway and as a learner driver close to my test I was 100% sure I'd handle it better than her. I kept wondering if I should beg her to pull over and let me drive the rest of the way, but of course that wouldn't have worked from an insurance point of view. I was so frightened I also seriously contemplated just asking to be dropped off at a fuel station and somehow making my own way back. But I was too locked into some ridiculous straitjacket of good manners and not wanting to offend her so I didn't. I can't express how relieved and grateful I was to finally make it home in one piece. After I'd had a stiff drink and a chance to calm down it struck me that at some point this erratic and unsafe driver had actually passed her driving test! We were around the same age, so it wasn't like she'd done it decades ago when standards weren't as high. I hadn't got my licence at that point but I knew I was already a much better and more responsible driver. I carried that feeling into my driving test the following week. I can remember thinking as I met my examiner, 'I deserve to pass' – and I did, first time, only one minor!' *Marcelle, 26*

CHAPTER 6:

HOW TO GET YOUR DRIVING TEST OFF TO A FLYING START

You know how when a day begins badly it tends get worse? For example sleeping through your alarm leads to spilling coffee on your clothes because you're in a hurry. You then have to change and miss the bus, arrive late at work or college and everything goes downhill from there.

Conversely we're all aware that when our day gets off to a good start, the rest of it has a tendency to go smoothly. That's why all those YouTube videos in which successful influencers describe their 'miracle morning' routine of meditation, cold showers and Acai berry smoothies are so popular.

It's exactly the same when it comes to your driving test. Getting the practicalities and your mindset prepared in advance will help you feel large and in charge, and ready to show your examiner what you can do.

Success checklist for the day before your driving test

Make sure you've got the admin sorted

You will need your provisional licence for your driving test and if you don't have it you'll be turned away. According to the DVLA over 1,100 driving tests a month get cancelled because candidates arrive in a car that doesn't meet the rules, are late for their test or bring the wrong paperwork. Don't let yours be one of them! Currently it's advised to take your Theory Test certificate but if you've lost it then the examiner can check the details of your pass online. However rules around the necessary paperwork for a driving test can change so always be sure to check the current situation on the government website.

Dress for success

Even if you don't usually lay out the clothes you're going to wear the night before, I'd suggest making an exception prior to your driving test, as it can help you feel more prepared and grounded.

Plan to wear whatever makes you feel most confident, whether that involves dressing up or down. If you look at photos of successful learners holding up their test pass certificates on driving instructors' social media pages, and use that as your style guide you'll see most are wearing clothes that are similar to ones they will have worn in their lessons, such as jeans and a jersey or T-shirt. When it comes to footwear it's definitely best to stick to familiar shoes or trainers that you've driven in previously.

If you wear glasses for driving place them where you'll find them easily tomorrow morning and if you've got long hair you'll need something to tie it back securely so the examiner has a clear view of your eye movements during the test.

Plan for punctuality

Many learners have their driving instructor pick them up from home for a practise lesson before their test. If that's what you have arranged then you can rely on your instructor getting you to the test centre on time. However if you're making your own way there I'd suggest giving yourself a very comfortable buffer when planning your journey so if there are any mishaps along the way you'll still be in plenty of time.

> I'd arranged to travel into town on the bus and meet my driving instructor at the test centre. But there was an accident and a diversion so I was 20 minutes late and missed it. Not only did I have the expense of another test but also for extra lessons to keep my skills up while I was waiting. I also had to pay for the use of my instructor's car again. The bill for that missed test ran into hundreds of pounds. I certainly made sure I got to my next one in plenty of time. *Fergus, 20*

Get into the zone

Definitely stay away from alcohol the night before your driving test. Its effects can linger in your system for hours and even if you're well under the limit you don't want to risk your reactions or mental clarity being affected in the slightest.

If, like most people, you feel somewhat anxious about your driving test it's best to make plans to spend the evening beforehand doing something uplifting, distracting or productive.

So for example, meeting friends, watching an enjoyable film, having a housework blitz or catching up with your to do list. Another option is to do something you know you're good at and find easy. Maybe playing a video game, cooking a great curry or taking photographs. It'll give you a feeling of success and accomplishment that you can carry forward into the following day.

One great stress-reliever is exercise. Running or swimming is excellent but what's even better is doing something which engages your mind as well as your body such as playing football or taking a dance class.

> I spent the night before my driving test cleaning and sorting out my bedroom. I'd been busy and it had become a complete tip. As well as hoovering and dusting I went on a de-cluttering binge, throwing out old college files and putting books and clothes I didn't want any more into a charity box. It distracted me and felt really satisfying as well. Waking up the next morning in a transformed room helped me feel positive and successful before I'd even got out of bed. And I went on to pass my test!' *Ella, 18*

> My driving test wasn't until late afternoon. I'd failed the first time because of nerves and I didn't want to get wound up by worrying about it so I went to the gym and did a workout. It went well so when I turned up for the test I was already feeling good about myself. Passed second time. *Nathan, 25*

Have a good night's sleep

One of the many benefits of exercise or productive activity such as cleaning is that it helps you fall asleep. Hopefully you'll be able to drift off without too much difficulty but if not you could use your wakeful state to practice calming visualisations. And don't worry if you find it difficult to nod off. One night's broken sleep won't make any difference to your driving performance or test result.

Success checklist for the day of your driving test

Start the day feeling positive

It's understandable if your first feeling on waking up is a sense of foreboding at the prospect of your test. But although that's perfectly natural, the trick is not to give 'driving test dread' too much attention. Remember your instructor wouldn't have put you forward if they didn't believe you were ready to pass and become a safe, independent driver. Now it's just a case of showing your skills to your examiner and getting that much-deserved licence. The only thing that can possibly get in the way is lack of self-belief and driving test nerves – and we're going to tackle them now.

Driving test nerves are no big deal

Yes, you feel nervous, but so what? So do most learners, and they go on to pass despite their sweaty palms, shortness of breath and butterflies in the tummy. The fact is that if the only successful candidates were those who took their test in a state of Zen-like calm, there would be very few drivers on the road. Accept your anxieties, whilst also realising that they needn't get in the way of your successful test pass.

My legs shook so much when I was walking over to the car for my first test, I wondered if I was going to just crumple onto the ground. They also trembled during the test, but not enough to affect my driving, thankfully. Somehow despite being incredibly nervous I still managed to do everything my driving examiner asked of me correctly, and passed. I was so grateful that I'd never have to go through that again, I cried with relief on the way home. *Amber, 30*

Visualise yourself succeeding and be inspired by other learners' success

Check out Chapter 2, Mindset Matters again for advice on crafting your own visualisations and affirmations for driving test day.

Maybe you could imagine the examiner turning to you and telling you you've passed. Or use an affirmation such as 'I am ready to pass my test today. I am ready to drive alone.'

Also, skip forward to Chapter 8, read the stories from successful learners describing their first drive alone and plan what yours will be!

Today is a good day visualisation

Not all visualisations have to be about the specific topic. You can shift yourself into a better mental and emotional state for your driving test without focusing on the actual event at all. Do the exercise below and see how much better it makes you feel.

Think of someone or something that you love. It could

be a family member, partner, friend, pet, new item of clothing, your motorbike, anything at all. Stretch out your arms while you're thinking of them (or it). You will find that you're smiling and your heart is warm Let that feeling expand and imagine yourself opening up to all the good things you want to experience today, and in your life. Now carry that feeling of happiness and optimism into your driving test.

Fuel the tank

We all have personal preferences when it comes to food, so eat whatever you feel is most likely to make you feel confident and grounded, whether that's a comforting bowl of porridge or a high-protein breakfast. Nerves often make people feel they can't face food at all, but if your test is later in the day do try to eat your regular meals, even if they are smaller than usual. If you've skimped on food you'll probably feel ravenous once your test is over so take a snack for afterwards.

Go easy on caffeine and sugary drinks, as you don't want to feel jittery. It's important to stay hydrated as when you're anxious you release the stress hormone cortisol. Drinking water will help dilute its effects and help you stay calm.

Eat a banana

This is one of the most popular pieces of driving test advice, and with good reason! Bananas are hailed as the driving test superfood. They are full of B vitamins, which help calm the nerves. Bananas also contain tryptophan, a type of protein that the body converts into seratonin, the 'happy hormone', which will keep your mood upbeat. And they're also high in potassium. When we're stressed our metabolic rate rises and potassium levels decrease. Eating a high-potassium snack like a banana will help rebalance the levels of this important mineral and normalise your heartbeat.

Take Bach Rescue Remedy

Rescue Remedy is made from plant flower essences and its aim is to provide calm and reassurance. There's no scientific evidence that Rescue Remedy works but many driving test candidates say it has helped reduce their anxiety. Over the years, 'take Rescue Remedy' has become part of standard advice on countering driving test nerves, along with 'eat a banana'. If you'd like to give it a try, Bach Rescue Remedy is available at health food shops and many chemists. You take it by putting a few drops into a glass of water, or you can put it directly onto your tongue.

> I took Bach Rescue Remedy before my driving test and passed. It might have been the placebo effect, but I didn't care. I was very nervous and just feeling I was 'taking something that would help', helped. *Sabrina, 19*

Turn off your phone

Obviously you'll need to turn off your phone during your driving test, but I'd advise switching off sooner than that. A phone is like having a slot machine in your pocket. If it pings with good luck texts from family and friends that's great. But equally you could pick up a message or see some news that upsets you and affects your concentration. Better to go offline so you can focus completely on your test.

Stay calm at the driving test centre

When you're in the waiting room at the test centre it's good to have something to distract you from any nerves. As mentioned previously, it's best to avoid picking up your phone messages so maybe listen to music or take a book to read (maybe even this one!). Doing calming breathing exercises or visualisations is an excellent use of this time.

Once the examiners arrive and you are assigned one your test has begun. This is covered in the following Chapter 7, How to impress your driving examiner, so you'll know what to expect.

> Waiting at the driving test centre for the test to begin was the worst part. Much more stressful than the test itself. You could sense how nervous most of the candidates were. Some would be scrolling on their phones, whilst others would be having last-minute pep talks from their instructors. I was always the oldest candidate by decades and felt very self-conscious. It gets a lot easier once the examiners arrive and you make a start on the admin side, such as showing them your provisional licence. It feels good to move out of that sense of suspended animation and be actually doing something. *Jane, 58*

Finally, some words of advice from driving instructors and successful learners

I always say to my learners, 'I know you can do it, you just have to do it on the day'. *Danielle 56, driving instructor*

Remember the examiner isn't expecting you to be a perfect driver, just a safe and capable one. Take each road and direction as it comes and don't worry about anything that may happen later in the test, such as carrying out certain manoeuvres or going on a dual carriageway. Stay in the present and focus on the drive as it's happening. *Ravi 43, driving instructor*

I failed three times and twice was when I was attempting parallel parks. I rushed them and made mistakes. So when it comes to manoeuvres take your time and don't get flustered. *Jane, 58*

One tip I heard was to pretend you're a different character, such as an airline pilot – cool, calm and collected. I tried that on my second test and I did pass. *Kris, 21*

Don't think you're going to be as nervous throughout your test as you are in the beginning. After the first few minutes or so the anxiety fades and you become focused on the drive. *Sasha, 17*

I took five driving tests and there were times I wondered if I'd ever succeed. But when

I finally got my licence it was one of the happiest days of my life. So my advice is to forget about past failures and go into your test feeling positive. Because when you pass it will all have been worth it. *Kira, 19*

You can do it. Believe in yourself. *Ali, 18*

CHAPTER 7:

HOW TO IMPRESS YOUR DRIVING EXAMINER

Your driving instructor has put you forward for your test because they know you're ready to drive independently. Deep down you know that too. Now there's just one more person you need to convince.... your driving examiner.

Most candidates feel stressed about their test. But please don't let that shift into paranoia about your driving examiner, building them up in your mind into some terrifying ogre who would like nothing better than to fail you. That's absolutely not the case. The role of a driving examiner is to ensure that only safe drivers are awarded a licence. If they fail a candidate it's because they're not up to test standard or because nerves let them down on the day.

Basically driving examiners are just people doing a demanding and sometimes stressful job. Don't see them as the enemy because they're not. In fact the more positively you can feel about your driving examiner the more relaxed you'll be and the better your test will go. The saying, *When we seek to discover the best in others somehow we bring out the best in ourselves* comes in handy here.

Having followed the advice in Chapter 6, How to get your driving test off to a flying start, you'll have arrived at the driving test centre in plenty of time and with all your paperwork in order.

In the UK driving examiners are allocated at random and they normally assess seven candidates a day. You can't refuse the examiner you've been assigned without having your test cancelled and losing the fee. The only acceptable reason is if they are a friend or family member, so if you have someone close to you who works as a driving examiner let them know of your impending test so they can flag this up and ensure they're not allocated to you.

It's important to bear in mind that your relationship with your driving examiner can feel different from the one you'll have had with your instructor. Over time, you and your instructor will have got to know each other and they will have seen you in good times and bad. Their role has been to teach and support you. However the role of your driving examiner is to assess you and it can feel like a more formal dynamic.

At the beginning of the test your examiner will come into the waiting room, call your name and introduce themselves. Hopefully they will appear friendly and approachable but even if they seem stern don't let it rattle you. Smile and greet them in a friendly, confident manner. They'll want to deal with the admin side first and will ask to see your provisional driving licence and theory test pass certificate if you have it. Aim to keep these accessible so you can hand them over without having to rummage in your bag and potentially become flustered. You'll then have to sign a residency and insurance declaration and confirm the email you'd like your test summary sent to. The examiner will ask you if you want to have your driving instructor or a friend/family member to accompany you on the test. This is something you will have discussed beforehand so tell the examiner your decision.

In some instances your driving examiner's supervisor might sit in on your test to watch your examiner's performance. This might not be your ideal scenario but it's best to be philosophical and accept it. If you refuse your test can be cancelled and you'll have to book another test and pay again.

The most important thing to remember is that the supervising examiner won't be judging you as they'll be assessing your examiner. Just tune them out and focus on driving as well as you can. And at least you can comfort yourself with the fact that you're not the only one being tested!

> I'd decided to have my driving instructor accompany me on my third test and then there was the supervising examiner too. There were four of us in the relationship so it felt a bit crowded. I'd never driven in a car with anyone sitting in the back seat before and that felt strange as well. Thankfully I got so caught up in the drive I forgot about the pair of them – and I did finally pass. *Jane, 58*

The UK driving test begins with an eyesight test, followed by the 'show me, tell me' vehicle safety questions. They are relatively straightforward so hopefully you'll sail through these sections and that will help build your confidence. Then you'll move onto the driving part of the test that will last around 40 minutes and cover general driving ability, reversing your vehicle and independent driving.

There are three types of driving faults candidates can potentially make:

- – a dangerous fault – this involves actual danger to you, the examiner, the public or property
- – a serious fault (sometimes called a 'major' fault) - something potentially dangerous

- a driving fault (sometimes called a 'minor' fault) – not potentially dangerous, but if you keep making the same fault it could become a serious fault

You'll pass your driving test if you make no more than 15 'minor' faults and no dangerous or serious faults.

To chat or not to chat?

Driving examiners will often chat to candidates during the driving part of the test to set them at ease. This can be helpful, but not always. If you're nervous making small talk can feel like another pressure and some people don't like talking when they're driving. But it's not a problem. Just tell your examiner that you'd rather not talk much during the test. They will understand and not think less of you in any way.

If you do feel comfortable chatting talk about whatever topics come up naturally, though obviously stay away from anything that might make you seem unreliable. This isn't a time for oversharing about messy nights out.

Conversely, if you're planning on doing anything such as post-test motorway training, putting new driver plates or your car or doing anything else which will flag you up as someone who takes their commitment to safe driving seriously then that's something you might like to drop into the conversation.

My first driving test was just before Christmas and my driving examiner and I discussed holiday plans. I had a different examiner for the second in January and we talked about getting fitter and wanting to join a gym. I was happy to chat both times and think it helped me forget I was being examined. *Jacob, 42*

When I took my driving test I explained I'd rather not chat and the examiner was fine about it. That was over a decade ago and even now talking while driving doesn't feel easy. I'm someone who needs all their concentration for the road ahead. *Amber, 30*

Driving Test Dos and Don't's

Do try to take your test in a driving school dual-controlled car

Whether you take your test in dual-controlled car or your own car won't make any difference to the result. You will be judged purely on the quality of your drive. However I'd urge you to use your driving instructor's car if at all possible.

Being a driving examiner can be a stressful job. They know nothing about potential candidates. They don't know how many lessons they will have had, or even if they've had any professional tuition at all. But they still gamely have to take them out to navigate difficult junctions and fast-moving traffic. Turning up in your driving instructor's car will reassure your examiner that that you have already proved yourself capable of driving at test standard. Also, making the necessary arrangements and adjustments to your own car to ensure it's suitable for the test can be complicated. If you get them wrong the test will be cancelled but you will still be charged the test fee.

Do be aware of the rules around taking the test in your own car

There are a lot of rules around taking your practical test in your own car. There are obvious ones, such as it has to be roadworthy and properly taxed and insured. But there are plenty of others. For example, you'll need to contact your insurer and extend your cover to allow the vehicle to be used for a driving test. You'll need an extra interior rear-view mirror for the examiner and the car interior must be tidy and smoke free. There are other rules that it's important to check out on the DVLA website. Some cars can't be used on the test as they don't give the examiner the all-round vision they need, these include the Toyota iQ and Ford KA convertible. Contact the DVLA in advance to ensure your car is suitable for the test.

Don't jump to conclusions about your driving examiner

Many people assume that driving examiners are recruited from former driving instructors, but they're not. The job is open to anyone aged 23 or over who has held a UK or EU licence for over 3 years, who has shown aptitude and undergone the relevant training. So your examiner could be much younger than you expect – and if you're a more mature learner they might even be younger than you!

Also, if you've heard rumours about 'that grumpy driving examiner' at your particular test centre and their description fits that of the person you've been assigned, don't worry. All driving examiners have to have a similar pass rate to that of their colleagues so it won't affect your test result.

My mates all said there was this one examiner at our local test centre who would
never pass you. They called him 'Mr Fail'.
My examiner fitted his exact description,
so I did worry but I was determined not to
let it put me off. I drove as well as I could
and passed first time. So it just goes to show
you shouldn't believe everything you're told.
Ali, 18

Don't think that your driving examiner is judging you on a personal level

Driving examiners are highly trained and a key part of this
is to ensure they behave impartially towards all candidates.
So whatever your age or appearance, they will be focused
on assessing your driving skills, not you.

I get teased for looking a lot younger than
my age. My brother's friends all say I look
about 12! Normally it doesn't bother me but
in the run-up to my driving test I began to
stress out in case the examiner might think
I looked too immature to have a driving
licence. I told my instructor Emily and she
said it totally wouldn't be an issue and not
to worry about it. *Sasha, 17*

Do ensure anyone accompanying you knows the rules

If you choose to have your driving instructor sit in on
your test then you're all good. They will know exactly how

to behave. But if you choose to have a friend or family member to accompany you ensure they know that they have to stay quiet, keep their mobile phone on silent and not try to communicate with you via coughs, meaningful glances or in any other way. They are not permitted to film the test. The examiner will also tactfully inform them just before the test that they mustn't comment or interfere, but it won't do any harm to flag it up beforehand.

Do switch off your mobile phone

Neither you nor your examiner want to hear a novelty ringtone or pinging social media notifications when you're trying to negotiate a busy junction. And bear in mind you're even more likely to receive calls and messages around the time of your driving test, as friends and family get in touch to wish you luck. Also, it might make your examiner think that you're the sort of person who would answer their mobile phone when driving, which is illegal.

Don't do the examiner's job for them

Don't waste energy trying to judge how the test is going or try to work out whether you've passed or not. That's the examiner's job. Drive as well as you can for as long as you can, and never stop trying. If you've made a serious fault you can't change that but you can avoid any future ones. And the fewer faults you have on this test, the more confidently you will go into the next.

> I stalled at a junction early on in my test and assumed I'd failed. When we got back to the test centre and my examiner said

I'd passed I was so surprised. But he said I'd done everything correct in the circumstances to make the car safe and restart it, so it wasn't an issue. *Sabrina, 19*

Do ask if you don't understand

If you don't hear or understand something your driving examiner has said then just stay calm and ask them to repeat or clarify their instructions. It is their duty to ensure that instructions are clear and understood by the test candidate so they will be keen to help you.

Don't worry when your examiner makes notes on their tablet

Your examiner will record your test details electronically on their tablet. They will note data such as the exact time you leave the test centre, whether your instructor is accompanying you, the route taken, and when you do certain exercises, such as completing a reversing manoeuvre. So don't assume the worst every time they write something down.

My driving examiner made several notes on her tablet before we'd even left the test centre. I immediately assumed she was writing down faults and that I'd failed already. She made notes throughout the drive and each time I was convinced it was yet another fault. But I was determined to do my best and drove as well as I could. When we got back to the test centre it turned out I'd passed with only two minors! *Dan, 18*

Do try not to feel too self-conscious

It can feel very off-putting to have someone closely monitor your every move, even down to your eye-movements. So it's completely natural to feel awkward knowing your examiner is observing you so closely. Even drivers with years of experience can be uncomfortable being watched, such as when they're doing a tight parallel park with a passenger they don't know well beside them. The answer is to accept the uncomfortable feeling but to also distract yourself from it, by focusing on the drive.

> I absolutely hated being observed during my driving tests. I was fine in written exams because I knew that if I wrote down something incorrect then I could cross it out, but in a driving test, if you hesitate or pull out too quickly at a junction it's game over. *Chloe, 42*

> I'm training as a hairdresser and we're always being observed by our tutors when learning new techniques so being watched by my examiner wasn't really that bad. *Ella, 18*

Don't get over-emotional

If other drivers behave badly, such as tailgating or cutting you up, keep your cool rather than acting annoyed. You need to show your examiner you can stay calm regardless of what else is happening on the road.

And if you feel you've made a mistake don't draw attention to it by apologising or muttering curses under your breath. Under stressful test conditions it can be difficult to have a true sense of what's really going on and your perceived mishap may only have been a minor fault, or maybe even not have registered as fault at all. Put it behind you and keep driving.

Don't flirt

In the distant past, when dinosaurs roamed the earth (also known as the 1970s and 80s) there was a rumour going around that flirting with your driving examiner would win them round and guarantee you a pass. This never made sense, even at the time. After all, if the examiner really found you that alluring, surely they'd be more inclined to fail you, in the hope of seeing you again? But anyway, it didn't work then and it certainly wouldn't work now so put the idea firmly from your mind and concentrate on your driving.

Don't bother wheeling out any sob stories

When chatting with your examiner you might be tempted to drop into the conversation that you desperately need to pass because you're about to start a new job/give birth/ have to drive your grandmother to hospital or whatever. But no matter how much sympathy your examiner might personally have for your plight they can't allow themselves to be influenced by it in the slightest and can only judge you on the quality of your driving.

Don't ask to end the test early

Sometimes candidates make a major, very obvious fault such as mounting the kerb early on in their test and feel that as they've clearly failed, they may as well suggest just driving back to the test centre. Don't do this! You've paid for your test so you may as well get the most out of it. Completing it under examination conditions will still be a hugely worthwhile experience for you, and stand you in good stead for your next test.

> I was very anxious before my first driving test and got into a real state with my nerves. Five minutes in I went over a stop line on a pedestrian crossing. I've never done anything like that before or since as I'm very cautious driver. I always assumed that if I failed it would be on hesitancy or failed manoeuvres. I felt upset but drove as well as I could after that. By the time we'd got back to the test centre I'd only made two more driving faults. I was disappointed but having completed the test meant I no longer saw it as some terrifying venture into the unknown. I knew exactly what it involved and that I could handle it. Next time I passed easily. *Maura, 25*

Don't do or say anything that could be mis-construed as a 'gift or bribe'

Driving examiners must report anyone who offers a 'gift or bribe' before, during or after test. Now I'm sure you're fully well aware that slipping your examiner an envelope stuffed with money isn't going to get you that test pass and wouldn't dream of doing it anyway. But it's still important to be cautious. Don't say anything that could even remotely be misconstrued as a bribe. For example, if you run a restaurant don't suggest they should drop by for a meal sometime in case it's misinterpreted as an offer of a freebie.

If you're someone who likes to give gifts, it might occur to you to offer your examiner a gift after a successful pass, but as stated earlier, the examiner will then be required to report you. A delighted 'thank you!' will suffice.

IF THE DRIVING EXAMINER HAS TO INTERVENE OR YOUR TEST HAS TO BE TERMINATED

Driving examiners must not intervene in your driving test except where it is necessary for public safety including that of themselves and the candidate. This is done by warning, advice or taking over the controls.

Your examiner will also intervene if they ask you to pull up by the side of the road and you choose somewhere it's illegal or unsafe to park.

The examiner can terminate the test if the candidate is behaving in an aggressive manner and sometimes tests need to be terminated because of illness. If you feel unwell during your test inform your examiner and the best course of action can be decided.

If the candidate is driving dangerously then the examiner will terminate the test and inform the candidate that they have failed. Neither you nor the examiner is permitted to drive the car back to the test centre but if your instructor is accompanying you they can do so. If not it's a case of walking, calling a taxi or getting someone to collect you.

Obviously this is a very difficult situation and you're going to feel shaken up. In the short term stay as calm as you can and focus on getting safely back to the test centre.

The reasons why this happened is something that can be worked through with your instructor at a later date.

At the end of your driving test

When you return to the test centre the driving examiner will ask you to turn off the engine and wait a few (excruciating!) moments until they complete their paperwork. They will then ask if you'd like your instructor or accompanying driver to listen to the test debrief. If you haven't had them along on the test, this is the time to call them over. It's best to have your instructor present as whether you've passed or failed you're likely to be feeling too emotional to take the information in properly.

You've passed!

If you've passed, the driving examiner will say those magical words that you have longed to hear '*That's the end of the test and I'm pleased to say you've passed....*'

You will probably be over the moon at this point, but be aware they will go on to give advice, '*Now that you'll be driving on your own I'd like you to be aware of...* ' and then give you any feedback they feel would be helpful.

They will then move on to the admin side of issuing your new (full, not provisional!) licence and sending you the full test report via email.

Even though you're now a licensed driver it's advisable for your ADI or someone else to drive you home so you have time to calm down before hitting the road unaccompanied. Before you do that it's important to read Chapter 8, You've Passed! Your First Drive Alone, for safety and insurance advice.

A failed test

If you've failed the driving examiner will say, '*That's the end of the test and I'm sorry you haven't passed. To help you I'll explain why*'. The feedback will cover all serious and dangerous faults, and if you've failed because of more than 15 driving faults, each one will be explained. If your instructor is present they will add, '*I am sure your ADI will be able to help you further*'. A copy of your test report will be emailed to you.

However upset you are try to stay as calm as possible. Listen to the feedback but don't argue or put yourself down. We can't help but pick things up subliminally, and you don't want an examiner (who may well be testing you again) hearing you say things like 'I failed on observations? Oh no, my instructor is always telling me off about those. I'm so easily distracted!' When the examiner has finished focus on holding it all together and say goodbye politely. It's usual for your ADI to drive you home afterwards so then you can allow yourself to be more emotional and cry or let off steam a bit.

Now isn't really the best time for any post-match analysis when it comes to where things went wrong. You can discuss it properly with your instructor during your next lesson and prepare for the next test together.

Challenging the test result

If you feel that the test result was unfair it is possible to challenge it. Full details of how to go about this are available on the DVLA website. However it's worth bearing in mind that if you succeed you don't get a test pass – just a refund of the test fee.

Threatening and abusive behaviour towards the driving examiner

Candidates who behave aggressively towards their examiner either during or after the test can be reported to the police. It could also take longer for them to get a future test as managers may feel they need two examiners present as a safety precaution.

Getting the same examiner for your second test

Getting the same examiner for your second test can be a real positive. After all, they're not an unknown quantity and this is an opportunity to show them how much you've improved.

> I was incredibly anxious during my first driving test. White-faced, sweaty palms gripping the wheel, too nervous to say more than a couple of words. I failed that test on an observation fault but had very few minors. After the initial disappointment I felt confident I'd succeed on my second test. As it happened I got the same examiner. She was lovely and we ended up chatting away. When the test was completed she told me I'd passed and also remarked on how much more confident I was, saying that, 'It was like driving with a completely different person'. *Lauren, 39*

Getting the same examiner for multiple tests

If an examiner has already failed you twice and you get them again, it can initially feel disheartening. But don't go down that road. The failure didn't happen because the examiner had anything against you personally, it was just the quality of your driving on the day. You're a lot more used to the test process this time round so you're less likely to be sabotaged by nerves or fear of the unknown. Now you can show the examiner what a capable driver you really are.

It took me eight attempts to pass my driving test. I was a capable driver but I've always had a tendency to go to pieces in exams. I had three tests with one examiner, one with another and four with the examiner who finally passed me. Over time we'd got to know each other reasonably well so it didn't feel as much like a 'test' as it had initially, which is probably why I managed to pass. *Sian, 26*

CHAPTER 8:

YOU'VE PASSED – AND YOUR FIRST DRIVE ALONE!

Passing your driving test is a magical moment in your life. You're going to want to celebrate with family and friends, bask in everyone's congratulations and of course take your first drive alone. But before that happens there are some important matters you need to sort out.

Getting your full driving licence

After informing you that you've passed your test and giving feedback on your drive your examiner will then make a start on the admin side of providing your full licence. It's very likely that at this point you'll feel over-whelmed by successful-test euphoria and not in the mood to be bothered with paperwork but what happens next is very important so do pay attention.

Your examiner will give you your driving test pass certificate. They will ask you if you would like them to take your provisional licence and arrange for the DVLA to send you your full licence through the post. This is the simplest route and if you take it your full licence should arrive within three weeks. If it takes much longer contact the DVLA. However, there are some reasons why you might want to hang on to your provisional licence. For example, if you need to use it as ID or if you've changed your name or address from the one currently recorded on your provisional licence. In that's the case then you'll need to apply for the full licence yourself. This involves filling out the DVLA form 'application for a driving licence' that you can get online or at post offices and sending it together with the required documents to their headquarters. This second route involves getting your paperwork organised but it's really important to crack on and do it. Because if you don't claim your full licence within two years of passing your driving test you'll have to take it again. And we wouldn't want that now, would we?

When can I legally drive alone?

While you're waiting for your full licence to arrive, your precious test pass certificate acts as legal proof that you're a qualified driver. And on the subject of your certificate, your instructor will probably want to take a photo of you brandishing it triumphantly beside their car so they can post it on social media and show off yet another happy and successful pupil. This is a special moment for both of you, so go for it.

Don't drive yourself back from the test centre

Although technically speaking it would be possible to sort out insurance on your phone and drive straight away, I'd strongly advise against it. You've just been through both the stress of your driving test and the elation of passing. Chances are, your emotions are all over the place. That's not the right state in which to tackle your first drive alone. Far better to be chauffeured back home or to work by your driving instructor or a family member or even to take the bus. One significant upside of this is that you can call and

message everyone en route with news of your triumph –
and you certainly wouldn't be allowed to do that if you
were at the wheel!

Three steps to your first successful solo drive

1. Sort out insurance cover

You need more than just your test pass certificate to legally
drive by yourself. You'll need car insurance as well. Professional ADIs and driving schools normally include the cost
of learner driver insurance during lessons in their fees. But
if you've been practising in your own car or one belonging
to a family member or friend then you will have had to
take out your own insurance. Any existing learner driver
policy will no longer be valid once you've passed your test
so contact your insurer, let them know you're now a fully
licensed driver and arrange your new policy. Unfortunately,
the cost of this may well be higher than the old one as it will
take into account the fact that you're now driving alone as
opposed to with a more experienced motorist beside you.

There's a lot to get to grips with when it comes to understanding car insurance and finding a policy that provides
the right cover at the best price. Hopefully you'll have
already done some research so the process won't be too
painful or lengthy. And do be sure to ask more experienced
and finance-savvy family and friends for advice as it'll
make the process a lot easier.

2. Don your P Plates (or equivalent) with pride

In some countries it's a legal requirement for new drivers
to wear special plates to alert other motorists that the car

is being controlled by a novice and they should drive with more care and consideration around them. For example in Northern Ireland you must use 'R' for 'restricted driver' plates for a year after passing your test. In Southern Ireland you must use 'N' for 'novice' plates for two years.

In England, Scotland and Wales new drivers have the option of 'P' for provisional plates. There's no legal requirement to wear them but road safety experts think it's advisable and I agree. It means that if you do make any errors of judgement in the early days as an independent driver, other motorists will spot your plates, realise you're a newbie and hopefully cut you a bit of slack.

3. Choose an easy first drive

We've all heard those 'I passed my test in Brighton in the morning and drove to Birmingham in the afternoon all by myself, no problem at all', stories. But frankly, when it comes to your first drive it's a good idea to lower the bar and choose an undemanding and familiar route that you can accomplish with the minimum of stress. Then over time you can build on that experience of success with more varied drives.

Many countries including Canada, Australia and New Zealand run a graduated licence system whereby new drivers will initially face certain restrictions around issues such as the times of day they are allowed to drive and the number or type of passengers they can have. So obviously if that's the case where you live then you will have to schedule your first drive to comply with the regulations.

But what if I don't have a car to drive alone in?

This state of affairs can feel very frustrating in an 'all dressed up and no-where to go' sort of way – but it's also surprisingly common. If all your learning has been focused on tuition with your instructor because you don't have a family or other car to practise in the fact you've passed your test isn't going to make a suitable vehicle magically appear. Many aspiring drivers' motivation for getting their licence isn't because they need to drive straight away but more because it's a skill they want to have sorted for their future. And if that's you by the way then congratulations. You've just made a very smart move.

If you want to keep your driving skills up to scratch but buying a car of your own isn't on your radar then being a named driver on a family member or partner's car might be an option. However, as you're newly qualified it's likely to bump up the cost of their insurance premium so you'll need to discuss how you'll both handle the finances. And if you're wondering whether car hire companies or car clubs might be an option, be aware that many companies have restrictions around age and don't hire out vehicles to anyone who hasn't had their licence for over a year.

If you don't have the opportunity to drive straight away you could find yourself in a situation that many ex-learners do, which is passing their test in their teens, going away to college and then much later needing to drive for work or commuting when they haven't been behind the wheel for years. In this instance it's always advisable to get refresher lessons to brush up your skills and increase your confidence.

Please take additional training – and stay safe out there

I'm fully well aware that after the hard work and expense of your lessons the last thing you're going to feel in the mood for is additional training of any kind. But according to the Royal Society for the Prevention of Accidents (RoSPA) one in five new motorists will be involved in a collision in their first six months of driving. This can be put down to causes such as inexperience, poor hazard perception and fatigue. There are still many aspects of motoring that you may not have experienced and top-up training will help enhance your skills. In the UK there's the Pass Plus course which is taught by suitably qualified ADIs. It has six modules including ones on driving in all weathers, on rural roads and in towns. Even if Pass Plus isn't something you're able to commit to currently then maybe you could choose a particular skill such as motorway or night driving and have an additional lesson focused on that.

And drive safely. Avoid alcohol completely if you're driving as even 'just one drink' can significantly affect your reflexes and judgement behind the wheel and increase your chance of being in an accident. Don't be distracted by your phone and if your mates start messing about when you're driving don't be distracted by them either. Just find somewhere safe, pull the car over and offer them the option of walking.

Your first drive alone

Having passed your driving test is a truly impressive feat and you deserve to be very proud of yourself. From your first drive alone onwards I wish you all the best for the future. Happy motoring!

My first drive wasn't anywhere exciting, just a commute to the shop where I had a Saturday job. But it was great to be able to put my handbag on the passenger seat because no-one else was sitting there and sing really loudly knowing no-one could hear me. *Sasha,17*

My parents' main reason for getting me through my test was so I could drive myself and my two younger siblings to school every day. That meant I didn't drive alone for the first week after passing. I asked if I could go out for a drive by myself but my mum said she didn't want me 'driving round for no reason wasting petrol'. Then we ran out of milk and I said I'd nip out and get some. So that was my first drive alone, a trip to the local super-market! It did feel great though. *Dan, 18*

It took me eight attempts to pass my driving test. My instructor, my partner and anyone else I went out practising with agreed I was capable but test nerves always sabotaged me. When I finally passed I couldn't wait to get out and drive alone. I went for a long trip through the countryside and what I especially loved was knowing I was could make my own decisions – I didn't have to second-guess what my instructor or an examiner thought I should be doing. We live in North Wales where road conditions can be hazardous, especially in winter, but

I've never had an accident and absolutely love driving now. *Sian, 26*

My nan said she'd give me her old Nissan Micra after I'd passed, but then she said she wanted to me to take her out in it first so she could check out my driving. So the day after my successful test I went over and she made me drive through town and we even had to go on the dual carriageway. If my nan felt I could have done something better she wasn't slow to correct me. The experience was way more stressful than being out with my driving examiner. But when we got back to her house she said that as a new driver I still had a lot to learn but overall I'd done very well. Then she got on the computer and messaged my parents and we all sorted out the transfer of ownership, car tax and insurance together. Afterwards I drove the 30 minute trip home in my own car. It was the best feeling of my life. *Ali, 18*

I'd promised myself that once I passed my test I would never drink and drive – not even an 'under the limit' glass of wine or beer. I would always stick to soft drinks. My first drive alone involved doing just that. I went out on the town with some girlfriends and because they'd always given me lifts in the past I offered to be the designated driver this time. We hit our favourite bars and instead of my regular Mojitos I found myself experimenting with non-alcoholic cocktails instead. Luckily there are some great ones out there and although not drinking felt strange at first, I realised what really mattered was enjoying the company of my friends. At the end of the night I got the other girls home safely and then drove home at 1am along the country roads. I felt very independent and proud of myself. *Millie, 26*

I went to the garden centre to stock up on bedding plants and compost. When my husband had his stroke we'd given up our car so for two years we'd managed with taxis and public transport. Passing my driving test meant we could both be much more independent. It also meant I could shop at the garden centre without having to limit myself to what I could haul back on the bus. *Jane, 58*

I live on Exmoor and my first drive was a few miles away to visit a friend. Some wild deer ran across the road just in front my car, but I was able to safely slow down and avoid them. It just proved that you always have to be alert. *Fergus, 20*

My first drive alone was to the restaurant where I work as a chef. But what was really special was driving home. Previously I'd end a shift feeling exhausted, then have to walk across town late at night to the bus station to catch a bus that would trundle through the suburban streets, taking ages. Now I was able to get into my car and be home in 20 minutes. Being able to travel home from work quickly and safely has made my life so much better. *Alex, 22*

I passed my test aged 19 and didn't drive again till I was 25 and moved out of London. I had a couple of refresher lessons then bought a second-car at a dealership on an industrial estate. I got there by public transport but had to drive back by myself. I didn't have a sat nav, got lost and then had to navigate a difficult junction before getting onto a busy dual carriageway. I hadn't even familiarised myself with the car's controls properly and am amazed I made it home in one piece. In retrospect I should have taken more refresher lessons and also either had my first car delivered or been accompanied by someone experienced. *Nathan, 25*

I passed my test on Monday, and despite having bought a new car I didn't go out in it until the weekend. That was because, having waited until my 40s to get my licence I wanted my first drive to be significant, rather than an everyday commute or shopping trip. On Saturday I drove to Scafell Pike, the highest mountain in England and climbed to the top. Then I descended at my own pace, got in my car and drove home. No need to car-share or fit around anyone else's preferences or timetable, just complete inde-pendence. My only regret was that I hadn't learned to drive sooner. *Jacob, 42*

My partner Lucy and I bought a car together. When I was learning I did most of the driving so I could practise as much as possible. Then when I passed I carried on being the main driver as I enjoyed it more. The only difference was Lucy wasn't officially 'super-vising' me any more and I could drive on the motorway. I still commuted to work on my motorbike because it was quicker, and so it was weeks before my first drive alone. It was very unexciting. I'd cleared out the garage and had to take some junk to the local recycling centre. I couldn't have done that on my bike. *Rowan, 23*

I just went for a general drive around the afternoon after passing my test. I kept to familiar streets with a 30mph speed limit. It felt quite weird and even eerie to be in the car by myself. Part of me kept wondering, 'am I really allowed to do this?' I was half-expecting to be pulled over by the police, despite the fact my pass certificate was lying on the passenger seat beside me. I remember whenever I stopped at traffic lights I'd do a deep exhale – meaning I must have been holding my breath the rest of the time. *Rukmini 33*

I passed my test months ago. I haven't driven by myself yet as I can't afford a car or insurance, or even to be insured on someone else's car. It's very frustrating because I love cars and wish I was out there driving now. But I'm still very proud of myself for getting my licence, and it's good to know that as soon as I get the opportunity, I can drive alone. *Ashley, 18*

My first drive was to visit my sister, who'd made a running joke of my inability to pass. I hadn't told her that I was learning again so arriving at her home in my new car was brilliant! *Chloe, 42*

I passed my test over twenty years ago, when I was working as a receptionist at a country house hotel which offered a service picking up guests from the railway station. My very first drive after passing was from my home to the hotel, about 5 minutes away. But my second was later the same day when my manager told me I had to go and collect some guests. The journey involved a short stretch of motorway which I was worried about but it went OK. They were a lovely elderly couple. I impulsively told them that I'd only just passed my test and they were my first passengers. They would have had every right to be worried but in fact they were very supportive and the gentleman even complimented me on 'a lovely smooth

drive' which did wonders for my confidence.
Lauren 39

I live in the middle of the countryside. The road between our house and the village is very winding and doesn't have a pavement so it's too dangerous to walk. Before I passed my test the only way I could get there was if my parents gave me a lift. They did their best but sometimes they were at work or looking after my younger sisters so they were too busy. There were times when I was desperate to hang out with my mates but felt trapped at home. My first drive was into the village to meet up with some friends and it felt like the most brilliant thing ever. At last I was free!' *Ella, 18*

A NOTE FROM THE AUTHOR

Thank you for reading Driving Test Secrets You Need to Know. I really hope you found it helpful. If you have a moment I'd be so grateful for an honest review, even if it's just a few words. Reviews are very important to authors and I read and appreciate every one. You can also find me at www.mariamccarthy.co.uk . I'm planning future books in the Driving Test Secrets series so do get in touch at maria@mariamccarthy.co.uk if you have any suggestions or feedback – and I'd love to hear about your own successful driving test pass!

For even more advice and support to help you pass your driving test check out www.drivingtestsecrets.com.

For more driving test tips and videos follow me on social media.

www.twitter.com/mariamccarthy11
Tiktok.com@drivingtestsecrets
www.facebook.com/drivingtestsecrets
instagram.com/drivingtestsecretsbook

Wishing you all the best on your journey to your successful driving test pass, and a future of happy and safe motoring.

Maria

Printed in Great Britain
by Amazon

41921841R00059